# Preparing a Catholic Funeral

## Rev. Kenneth Koehler

This guide is the result of my experiences in helping many of the parishioners of Most Precious Blood Parish in Denver, Colorado, plan for either their own funeral or the funeral of loved ones. Preparing a Catholic Funeral has been an extremely helpful resource in my parish. My hope is that it will help you as well.

Morehouse Education Resources
*A division of Church Publishing Incorporated*

Morehouse Education Resources
19 East 34th Street
New York, NY 10016

Morehouse Education Resources is an imprint of Church Publishing Incorporated.
www.churchpublishing.org

Cover Design: Laurie Westhafer

Scripture readings from the Order of Christian Funerals, approved for use in the dioceses of the United States of America by the National Conference of Catholic Bishops and confirmed by the Holy See (1998 edition), are taken from the New American Bible with Revised New Testament © 1986, 1970 Confraternity of Christian Doctrine, Washington, DC and are used by permission of the copyright owner. All Rights Reserved. "Answers to Ten Frequently Asked Questions," copyright by John Horan, "Honoring Wishes for End-of-Life Care" and "The Vigil Service: Sharing the Reality of Life and Death" copyright Dianne L. Josephson, "After Loss—Putting the Pieces Back Together" and "Seven Tips about What to Say and Do to Comfort Others" copyright Steven V. Malec are used with permission of the authors.

Printed in the United States of America

ISBN 978-1-60674-120-7

# Contents

# Foreword

*by Alan D. Wolfelt, Ph.D.*

For thousands of years, funerals have been a means of expressing our beliefs, thoughts and feelings about the death of someone we love.

The funeral ceremony…
❖ helps us acknowledge that someone we love has died.
❖ helps us remember the person who died and encourages us to share those memories with others.
❖ offers a time and place for us to talk about the life and death of the person who died.
❖ provides a social support system for us and other friends and family members.
❖ allows us to search for the meaning of life and death in the context of our faith.
❖ offers continuity and hope for the living.

One of the most important gifts of planning a meaningful funeral is that it helps family and friends to focus their thoughts and feelings on something positive. The funeral encourages them to think about the person who has died and to explore the meaning of that person's life and the ways in which she touched the lives of others. It is also a time and place for them to reaffirm their faith in new life after death.

The remembering, deciding and reflecting that takes place in the planning of the service are often an important part of the process of grief and mourning. And ultimately, this process of contemplation and discovery creates a memorable and moving funeral experience for all who attend.

Some time ago I created this layered triangle graphic to capture my philosophy of the Hierarchy of Purposes of the Funeral. Let's look at each layer in turn:

### Reality

When someone we love dies, we are faced with acknowledging a difficult reality. It is hard to truly accept the finality of death, but the funeral helps us begin to do so. At first we accept it with our heads, and only over time do we come to accept it with our hearts.

### Recall

Funerals help us begin to convert our relationship with the person who died from one of presence to one of memory. When we come together to share our memories, we learn things we didn't know and we see how the person's life touched others.

### Support

Funerals are social gatherings that bring together people who cared about the person who died. This reason for having funerals is especially important to remember if the person who died liked to say, "I don't want a funeral. Don't go to any trouble." Funerals are in *remembrance* of the person who died, but they are *for* the living. Those who loved the person who died need and benefit from having a special time to support one another in their grief.

Transcendence

Meaning

Expression

Support

Recall

Reality

### Expression

So many thoughts and feelings fill our minds and our hearts when someone we love dies. Collectively, these thoughts and feelings are what we mean by the term "grief." In other words, grief is what's inside us. When we *express* our grief—by crying, talking to others, sharing memories, taking part in a funeral ceremony—we are mourning. Mourning is grief communicated outwardly. When we grieve but do not mourn, our sadness can feel unbearable and our many other emotions can fester inside of us. Mourning helps us begin to heal. The funeral is an essential time for mourning.

### Meaning

Did the person I love have a good life? What is life, anyway? There are no simple explanations, but the funeral gives us a time and a place to hold the questions in our hearts and begin to find our way to answers that give us peace.

### Transcendence

Funerals have a way of getting us to wake up—to think about what we truly care about and how we want to spend our precious remaining days. Ultimately, funerals help us embrace the wonder of life and death and remind us to live deeply, with joy and love.

### Planning a Funeral is a Privilege

As you consider the funeral, try to remember that planning a funeral is not a burden, but a privilege. Think of the funeral as a gift to the person who died as well as his friends and family. It is a chance for all to think about and express the value of the life that was lived. It is also a chance to say goodbye.

This is not to deny the need of friends and family members to mourn and to embrace painful feelings of grief in the coming days. They may feel deep sadness as they plan this funeral and begin to acknowledge the reality of the death. But when all is said and done, all those involved in planning the funeral also feel deep satisfaction that they have helped plan a meaningful tribute. And those who loved the person who died begin to work their way from the bottom of the pyramid—acknowledging the reality of the death—to the top.

Planning and attending a meaningful funeral can have a lasting and profoundly important impact on the lives of so many people. Tapping into the power of ceremony assists them on their journey to transcendence.

### About the Author

Alan D. Wolfelt, Ph.D., is a respected author and educator on the topic of grief. He believes that meaningful funeral experiences help families and friends support one another, embrace their feelings, and embark on the journey to healing and transcendence.

Recipient of the Association of Death Education and Counseling's Death Educator Award, Dr. Wolfelt presents workshops across the world to grieving families, funeral home staffs, and other caregivers. He also teaches training courses for bereavement caregivers at the Center for Loss and Life Transition in Fort Collins, Colorado, where he serves as Director. He is also the author of many bestselling books, including *Understanding Your Grief*, *The Mourner's Book of Hope* and *Creating Meaningful Funeral Ceremonies*. For more information, visit *www.centerforloss.com*.

# How to Use this Booklet

This booklet is the result of one pastor's attempt to help those who must face the often unfamiliar task of preparing a Catholic funeral. It is designed to manage the many practical details that go into planning a Catholic funeral and to help gather the information that will be of help for the survivors, the mortuary, the cemetery and the parish.

This booklet may be used either by those who have just experienced the death of a loved one or by those who wish to decide in advance about the many details of their own funeral. These advance decisions allow that, when death does occur, the survivors will have a record of the deceased's wishes and will be able to plan the funeral liturgy in a way that respects these wishes.

This booklet has been created to ensure that the practical details connected with planning a funeral are attended to in a way that helps all involved make the funeral a suitable celebration of the special meaning of the deceased person's life.

### Using the Instruction Forms

At the end of this booklet, there are forms that may be completed, torn out, copied and given to one's relatives, personal representative or attorney, the mortuary and the parish church to keep on file. The information and instructions on these forms will be helpful for making the funeral plans. It is important to contact the cemetery, the mortuary and the parish where the funeral will be celebrated to finalize these plans before the funeral is to take place.

# Coping with Death

## Preparing for Death

*by Rev. Kenneth Koehler*

### When Death Is Near

When someone faces death or is critically ill, the family members should immediately contact a priest and not wait until death is imminent. The sacrament of the Anointing of the Sick is for those preparing for death or facing a critical illness. Celebrating this sacrament encourages the sick or dying person through the experience of the healing presence of Christ, whose resurrection offers hope for a new life beyond suffering and death.

If the situation allows, this is an appropriate time for loved ones to ask about the dying person's wishes for the funeral celebration, for example, by using the forms found on pages 47-56 of this booklet if they have been filled out in advance. It is also helpful to ask whether any prior arrangements might have been made for someone to make decisions for the sick person (for example through a durable power of attorney or a living will), for organ donation, for the burial plot, vault, marker or niche for cremated remains in a cemetery or for prepaid funeral plans.

### When Death Occurs

When a loved one dies, the family should call the priest from the person's parish. Since the sacrament of the Anointing of the Sick is for the living, the priest would not anoint the deceased person but would pray with the family in the presence of the body for the eternal salvation of the deceased and for the consolation of those who are gathered.

If no choice of a cemetery and mortuary has been made, the hospital or nursing home where the death took place will assist the family or responsible person to choose and contact a cemetery and a mortuary. Should the death take place at home, then the family should consult any available records indicating the deceased's wishes or any prior arrangements with a cemetery and a mortuary. Otherwise, they should choose a cemetery and a mortuary whose reputation they trust. If a cemetery and a mortuary have already been chosen, then it will be necessary to contact the cemetery and the mortuary. There is a form at the end of the booklet (see p. 51) to gather the information that the mortuary would normally request.

# After Loss—Putting the Pieces Back Together

*by Steven V. Malec, BBA, NCBF, national speaker and Director of Bereavement Ministry for the Catholic Cemeteries Association in the Diocese of Cleveland, OH*

Life and death are partners. At some point, all of us will face death: our own as well as those we love. To lose a loved one through death always causes changes for us and for our lives. Life is about change. Sometimes it is painful. Sometimes it is beautiful. Many times it can be both.

After the overwhelming loss of a loved one, it feels like your heart—and your entire world—is completely shattered into pieces. No one asks for life to change this way, but it does. We have no control over death, but we do have control over how we respond to death. How we respond is what counts. After a loss, we find out who we are as we go about putting the pieces of ourselves and our lives back together.

### The First Piece: Recognize the Loss

If grief is to be healed, it must be identified, acknowledged, felt and expressed. Grief only destroys us when we deny it or refuse to deal with it. Admit and honor your feelings of loss. The psychologist and spiritual writer Henri Nouwen counsels that "The only feelings that do not heal are the ones you hide." Therefore, the only cure for grief is to grieve. It is as simple and as difficult as that.

To begin grieving, you need to accept the full reality of your loss—in both the big and all the little ways. The primary loss is that of your loved one; however, there are always a host of other losses as well. You need to identify all the losses that the death of your loved one involves. Make a list and identify all your losses so you know exactly what you are dealing with.

### The Second Piece: Express the Loss

Initially, a very important step in the healing process is to tell and retell the story of your loss, with all of its pain. We need to experience the pain and express it in order to heal. Pain and emotional feelings are essential ingredients in the healing process.

Sharing your loss helps to ease that pain. You can share your loss by talking, writing, crying and praying. Grief is not a problem that we fix or solve, but an experience that we must embrace and express in order to heal.

Grieving is not something that must be done alone either. Ask for help from your family, friends, church and professional agencies. Don't always wait for others to read your mind and offer help. Make a list of what you need and be willing to accept the help that others offer. Be gentle and patient with yourself and realistic with what you can and simply cannot do at this time. Keep in touch with supportive friends or others who have been in a similar situation. Think about attending a support group.

### The Third Piece: Learn about Grief

Grief is the normal, natural and appropriate response to the loss of a loved one. It is essential for the healing process. You are not going crazy; you are grieving. You work through the loss of a loved one by moving from the deep pain, intense sorrow and distressing regret to healing, inner peace and even joy.

It helps to learn all you can about the grief process. Read literature on grief and loss and watch the newspaper for articles about grief. Check with your church for support and resources. Look up Websites that have information on grief. Get on the mailing list for bereavement care newsletters from your cemetery, funeral home and area hospice.

### The Fourth Piece: Face Your Loss

As you grieve, you are going to hurt. Grieving means living with pain. But that pain is the sign that you loved someone and someone loved you. You will always miss them and long to hear their voice one more time and that is okay. You cannot heal what you do not allow yourself to feel. Over time, each day will get a little better.

Each person's experience of loss is unique, but there are also common elements of grief. There is no right or wrong way to grieve, no orderly stages of progression. There are, however, healthy and unhealthy ways to cope with your grief.

Some healthy ways of coping include: talking about your loss with family, friends and others, writing in a journal, prayer, visiting the grave, looking at photos, honoring your feelings and taking good care of yourself physically and spiritually.

Doing these things often brings lots of tears. For both women and men, crying is a natural response to sorrow and can be extremely healing. Crying supports the immune system. Scientists have discovered that tears of sadness are chemically different from tears of joy. Crying these tears of sorrow flushes out depressants from the body.

You must also learn how to deal with the pain of your grief. The death of a loved one is the greatest of hurts that you will ever endure, and healing is never easy. Grieving takes courage, patience, endurance and faith. And though grieving is healthy and necessary, still it takes a huge toll on your body, mind and soul. So make sure to get proper rest, nutrition and exercise.

### The Fifth Piece: Work through Your Grief

Grief has many different names and faces. When grieving a loss, it is normal to experience any of the following: shock/disbelief/numbness; loneliness/emptiness; fear/anxiety; anger/hostility; deep sadness/situational depression; a lack of purpose; a lack of energy; inability to concentrate; change in eating habits; change in sleeping habits; guilt/regret/relief; searching; envy of others; a strengthening or weakening of faith; acceptance/survival/healing.

Be determined to take time, notice and work through your grief even if others may want to hurry you through it. The funeral and burial may be finished in a week, but grieving goes on for a much longer time. The initial grief reactions of shock and disbelief are not the most painful or enduring ones. The five main grief reactions that usually remain the longest are anger, guilt, fear, sadness and loneliness. As you work through your grief, these acute grief reactions often lessen in intensity and soften. But you will have feelings of grief and will keep having them until you no longer need to.

There comes a time in your grief process when you will need to press through your emotions and grief reactions. Do not allow the "whys," the guilt or the regret to paralyze you in your grieving. If you do become stuck in your grief or if there is an issue that you cannot resolve, you may want to seek professional help. Also, let your faith help to heal you—in prayer give these unresolved areas to God as a seed and you will discover that God will bring you a harvest.

### The Sixth Piece: Manage Your Loss

There is no easy way to bypass the experience of grief when a loved one dies. You must learn to manage your loss and not have your loss manage you. Bad things do happen to good people. You are still fragile, yet strong. Your heart is shattered, your bones ache and there are knots in your stomach.

Time alone does not heal all wounds, but rather what you do with your time does. Your heart is deeply wounded, and it will take time and hard work for healing to occur. While there is no set time schedule for the grief process, research shows that most grief reactions will be experienced and healed within 2-4 years for an anticipated loss and 4-7 years for a sudden loss. Although we usually want to know how long our grief will last, it is better to ask how willing are we to accept the reality of pain and truly work toward healing it.

Gradually, you will not only reclaim aspects of your old life but also add new ones, too. You will never really "get over it," but you can get through it. Through grieving, "moving on" is really moving back to former activities that you used to do and enjoy—dining out, going to the movies, doing hobbies, shopping, singing in church, among others.

We never really "let go" of our loved ones, but we do loosen our grip a little bit and let go of some of the pain. They are still a part of you and always will be! Take time to make a little connection with them every day.

### The Seventh Piece: Hope for Healing

At the root of our faith is an unshakeable hope. Death is not the end. We believe that with Christ, there is life after death—"for your faithful people life has changed, not ended" (Preface of Christian Death, 1). Knowing and experiencing this makes our grief much different. It may not be any easier, but it is different.

We are like the Israelites who, when faced with the destruction of Jerusalem and its temple, did not despair but dared to hope and cried out in their grief: "My soul is bereft of peace; I have forgotten what happiness is. My soul continually thinks of my affliction and is bowed down within me. Yet I still dare to hope when I remember this: the steadfast love of the Lord never ceases, his mercies never come to an end" (Lamentations 3:17, 20-22).

We too dare to hope in the Lord. When a loved one dies, we grieve their loss. Christians grieve like everyone else, but we also grieve with faith and look to the crucified and risen Jesus for our hope. St. Paul encourages us to trust in the power of Christ's resurrection: "We do not want you to be uninformed, brothers and sisters, about those who have died so that you may not grieve as others who have no hope. For since we believe that Jesus died and rose again even so, through Jesus, God will bring with him those who have died" (1 Thessalonians 4:13-14).

There is life after death for your loved one. There is also life after loss for you! After the death of a loved one, your life has been changed because of your loss. Over time, your grief will change, too. It will soften. You will not always feel as you do at this moment.

But just because your life has changed, this doesn't mean it is ruined. There is hope and healing. First you must allow yourself to feel the pain of loss and grieve. Then in time and with hard work, the good days will begin to outnumber the bad days.

Let faith be your consolation and eternal life your hope. Jesus can help you heal if you invite him into the process. Through Jesus' suffering and death, we find hope and healing. It is an unrealistic expectation, however, to think that healing will restore your life back exactly the way it was before your loss. There is no full recovery. Some part of your loss may remain unrecovered for the rest of your life.

This doesn't mean that you cannot have peace and joy within you. Healing involves making peace with your life and even finding joy again. There is always loss before gain. Through this healing process, you will emerge a new person— stronger, more compassionate, more understanding and loving, with a life full of renewed meaning, purpose and love.

### Putting the Pieces Back Together

Although this life has to end, love doesn't. A heart can be broken; but it still keeps beating. You can feel shattered, but you can put the pieces together again. Healing is a daily journey and a constant choice to go on and to look forward. Healing comes not from the forgetting, but from the remembering. Piece by piece, you will be healing.

May you experience the peace of Jesus Christ, which is beyond all understanding, as you journey through your loss to healing and anticipate your joyful reunion with all your loved ones.

# Ashes to Ashes, Dust to Dust, Q & A: Catholic Funeral Practices

*by Roxanne King, Editor, Denver Catholic Register*

*"For dust you are, and to dust you shall return."*
— *Genesis 3:19*

The *Denver Catholic Register* spoke with Deacon Charles Parker, director of the archdiocesan Office of Liturgy, about Catholic funeral practices.

**Q:** What does the Catholic Church teach about death?

**A:** It's a transition from life to new life. In the prayers for the funeral Mass it says when our earthly dwelling ends in death we gain an everlasting life in heaven.

**Q:** What does the Church say about care of the body after death?

**A:** One of the reasons we use incense at the funeral Mass and incense the casket that houses the body is we believe the body is the temple of the Holy Spirit; through baptism and confirmation we know that Christ resides in our body. So that's why we owe the greatest honor and respect to the body in this life and after death.

**Q:** Both burial and cremation are permitted for Catholics. Which is the preferred option and why?

**A:** The Church clearly says that while cremation is permitted it doesn't enjoy the same value as burial of the body. In the new appendix to the Order of Christian Funerals for the cremation rite, it says the Church prefers and urges that the body be present for the funeral rites if one does choose cremation, but the Church says that cremation doesn't hold the same value as burial of the body. Just as Christ was bodily buried in the tomb, so ought we to follow that example.

**Q:** Do cremated remains need to be buried?

**A:** Cremated remains need to be treated with the same respect as we would the body of our deceased loved ones. They need to be inurned into the ground or placed in a cremation niche, which is the same for cremation as a mausoleum is for the body. The practice of keeping your loved one around the house is not the reverent disposition the Church requires. Nor is the scattering of ashes allowed. The cremated remains are to be buried or placed in a mausoleum-type niche.

**Q:** Why is it important not to scatter the remains?

**A:** The Church says the scattering of remains is not the reverent disposition that the Church requires; we need to treat them as we would a body. We would never think of parting out the body of our loved ones, nor should we part out their remains.

**Q:** What are the three stations of a Catholic burial?

**A:** The three principal stations of Catholic burial are: the funeral vigil—some people opt for a rosary—followed by a funeral Mass and, lastly, the prayers of committal done at the gravesite. Those are the three principal stages of Christian burial. There are additional options. There are options for the family to gather with a priest or deacon in the presence of the body and do initial prayers at first viewing at the mortuary. There are options for praying the office of the dead. There are many different options, just as there are for the funeral, to mark this journey with our loved ones from this earth to new life.

**Q:** What is and isn't permitted regarding music for a Catholic funeral liturgy?

**A:** Funeral music has to be sacred, liturgical music—particularly if the liturgy is in a church, in a sacred space. The music for a funeral Mass or rosary or vigil service held in a church must be sacred liturgical music. A good rule to follow is that if you don't hear a particular piece of music on Sunday in a Church, you won't hear it at a funeral Mass. If a family chooses to have a rosary or vigil service at a mortuary chapel, which is non-sacred space, there is a little more freedom for non-liturgical music to be used, but it must still be of the proper decorum and not anything contrary to Christian values.

**Q:** Are all cemeteries blessed?

**A:** No. Catholic cemeteries are blessed ground. A Catholic can be buried in other grounds, which are not blessed ground, but if they are buried there, the priest or minister or a lay minister, if they lead the burial rite, has a prayer of blessing for the grave.

**Q:** Can non-Catholics be buried in a Catholic cemetery?

**A:** Non-Catholics can be buried in a Catholic cemetery. Oftentimes the Liturgy Office receives calls from someone who wants to bury such a person and they want a funeral Mass. It is permitted, as long the deceased would not have objected to it.

**Q:** What is one of the most frequent questions your office gets about Catholic funeral practices?

**A:** The one thing people should keep in mind is there is a balance between honoring the wishes of the dead and having rites and rituals that the Church has provided that bring meaning to the family that's living. So people should let their funeral wishes be known. Oftentimes family members have no idea what their mom or dad or grandma or grandpa would want. Letting people know beforehand reduces the stress of trying to bury someone. It's a very difficult task to bury someone: we ask people to pick readings, pick music and decide on various other things at the mortuary. Ultimately, we as Catholics are living for the grave—it's only through the grave that we come to know and live in the presence of God. Therefore, we should approach funeral planning and our death with confident assurance and hope and plan it as another part of our life's journey.

**Q:** Is there anything else you would like to add?

**A:** With the popularity of cremation it is important to know that if your loved one is cremated before the funeral Mass, there are some distinctions in the ritual. For example, while the cremated remains are greeted in the back of the church, like the body would be, there is no funeral pall for the urn—the funeral pall that symbolizes the baptismal garment. The prayers at graveside and at the sprinkling with holy water are a little different. It's important for people to know that the preference of the Church is to celebrate with the body, then cremate following that, then burial. Mortuaries can help people understand that in that case they do not buy a casket; they can rent or loan one for that use.

Reprinted with permission of the *Denver Catholic Register*, published by the Archdiocese of Denver and originally printed in the November 12, 2008 issue. Visit *http://www.archden.org/index.cfm/ID/8307/DenverCatholicRegister*

# Preparing Children for Funerals

*by Rev. Kenneth Koehler*

Often people want to "protect" children from the harsh reality of a death. Yet the child is part of the family for whom death causes a major change in their lives. So children should be drawn into discussions regarding the death and the funeral planning. Adults often resist allowing children into this conversation because adults fear not being able to answer children's questions. But experts recommend this involvement to help both adults and children with their grieving.

Communication about death is easier when a child feels that he or she has our permission to talk about a subject often not talked about, especially with children. We must deal with the inescapable fact of death, and so must our children. To help them, let them know that it is okay to talk about it. In fact, any discussion with the children will also aid adults in their own grief process.

Death should be explained to a child as simply and directly as possible by someone very close. Listen carefully to the child and consider the child's feelings about this particular death or about death in general. Adults need to realize that the child's understanding of death always depends upon his or her age, maturity and intelligence.

Children from ages three to five usually know very little, if anything, about death. But since they are very curious, they can have many questions that should be answered as simply, directly and truthfully as possible, especially without suggesting that death is reversible or has not really happened.

Children from ages five to nine have begun to understand that death is final, and their questions can often be harder to answer. But again, direct and truthful answers will help them confront the reality of death and cope with their own grief.

Older children, ten through the teenage years, might recognize death's inevitability and also realize it could happen to them. Anger and guilt feelings can also occur in relation to a death, especially one within their family, friends or peer group. It is important to communicate that they were in no way responsible for the death.

When a death occurs, the children should be given the news in a way that gives them time to ask questions and includes them in the emotional experience of the whole family. They are an important part of the family and should be included when the family celebrates and grieves together.

Whether or not a particular child should be included in the funeral depends upon the child and the situation. If he or she is asking questions about the death, then they are probably old enough to be present at all the events of the wake and funeral. If the child is old enough to understand and wants to participate, being included may help accept the reality of death and offer a way to express grief in the company of family and friends. If a child prefers not to attend the funeral, it is not wise for the child to be coerced or made to feel guilty.

If a child is to attend a funeral, preparation should be given beforehand about what will be seen and heard before, during and after the service. Children often feel unsure about their social skills and have difficulty trying to figure out what to say and do. Help the child understand that on such sad occasions, no one ever has just the right words of consolation for the survivors. Let the child know that at the funeral people will also be expressing their sorrow in various ways and many will be crying, which is a very appropriate expression of sadness and grief when a loved one dies.

If children need more assistance in answering their questions, parishes, funeral directors or cemeteries often have bereavement resources that can be used to help children understand and cope with their experience of death. Remember that not only for adults but also for children, healing will take time and continuing support to help them through the grieving process.

# Honoring Wishes for End-of-Life Care

*by Dianne L. Josephson, RN, MSN, author, educator, consultant and Director of the Healing After Loss Ministry at St. Pius X Parish, El Paso, TX*

### Human Life Is Sacred

From the moment of conception to that of natural death, human life is sacred. The joy of a new life coming into the world is openly discussed and celebrated, yet we often shun the "uncomfortable" topic of death. Death, however, when openly embraced as a natural part of the life continuum, can be one of the most beautiful and spiritual moments of our lives.

Jesus presented us with the finest model of how to confront death with dignity, fortitude and hope. Throughout his life, he taught us how to understand death in the context of love, compassion, forgiveness, peace and the assurance of eternal life. As followers of Christ, we are called upon to imitate Christ when we comfort the sick and the dying, walk with those who are grieving, embrace our own mortality and prepare for our journey home to God. With advance planning, we validate life and accept the inevitability of death.

### Needs of the Dying

When we fully acknowledge our mortality and embrace death, we also take care of the common needs that confront us at the end of life. These encompass all aspects of our legacy, including making financial plans, drawing up a will to provide for those we leave behind, writing advance directives to help ease the burden on loved ones when we can no longer address our own care and providing a durable power of attorney to ensure that our wishes are followed in the event that we are too incapacitated to make our own medical decisions.

### Advance Directives and Durable Power of Attorney

Advance directives include a living will (or medical directive) and a durable power of attorney for health care (or healthcare proxy). When writing advance directives, people often choose a combination of these. Since laws vary from state to state regarding advance directives, it is wise to contact an estate attorney to determine specifics for a particular state. Costs vary for such services, especially when dealing with a complex estate. The cost, however, is very much worth it and avoids expensive and drawn-out legal battles for survivors.

Without an advance directive, some of the hardest and most important decisions of a person's life can be left entirely in the hands of medical professionals, family members or the state. An advance directive is legal in every state, and most hospitals will allow a person to keep a copy of an advance directive on file with them. Having an advance directive on file can help ease a person's fear about what will happen once admitted to a hospital for treatment or end-of-life care.

Advance directives decide ahead of time what medical procedures a person does or does not want. They often include decisions about pain control, breathing machines, intravenous or gastric delivery of medications, fluids and nutrients, cardiopulmonary resuscitation and organ donation. They also assist family members in making very difficult decisions while ensuring that a person's expectations are followed when these might be different or opposed to those of family members.

A durable power of attorney for health care, which is different from a regular power of attorney, gives another person the power to make healthcare decisions for us. In it, we designate someone to make medical decisions for us if we become too ill or unable to make them. Healthcare providers and legal advisors encourage that, regardless of a person's health status or age, one have a living will and, more importantly, a durable power of attorney for health care.

### Death with Dignity

When we come to terms with the inevitability of our own death, then it is important to be as detailed as possible regarding the circumstance of our death. We all want to die with dignity but it is up to us to attend to the details.

We are the only ones who can honestly make choices regarding our own end-of-life care. It is important to thoroughly think through what we want and don't want, discuss these desires with trusted loved ones or friends and then write them down in a legal document, as described above. It is our life and we need to state clearly the way we want to die.

In doing these things, we also show our love for family by relieving them of the burden of decision making. It is never too early to discuss and make these decisions. We must not wait until a health crisis occurs.

Each one of us needs to address questions such as:

❖ What are my fears about dying?
❖ What are my fears about losing control of my mental and bodily functions?
❖ If I were to become very ill (cancer, disabling stroke, unconscious) what type of medical care and treatment would I want/not want?
❖ Would I want to be kept comfortable with pain control or would I prefer to be kept alive as long as possible on machines?
❖ What are my feelings about pain management?
❖ Do I want to remain alert, even if it means I have some degree of pain, or would I prefer to be totally free of pain, regardless of my state of consciousness?
❖ If I could no longer swallow, would I want feeding tubes and intravenous supplements?
❖ Would I want my life prolonged by the technology of machines if I could no longer think for myself, become comatose or terminally ill and near death?
❖ Who would I want to take care of me (family, health professionals)?
❖ Where do I want to die (at home with hospice care, in a hospital or a long-term care facility)?
❖ Who do I want to make decisions for me?
❖ Do I want to donate my organs?
❖ Do I want an autopsy?
❖ What do I want for the final disposition of my body (burial, cremation, other)?
❖ What kind of funeral service do I want?
❖ How do I want to be remembered?

Once we have thoroughly and honestly considered and answered these questions, it is time to act on them. When steadfast regarding our personal beliefs and desires, then only can we approach a spouse, parent, child or other trusted individual about what is best for us. The choice is ours.

By facing death, and preparing for it physically, emotionally and spiritually, we can live out our days in peace. As followers of Jesus Christ, we give testimony to his life and death and find our hope by trusting in his resurrection. Then, with a sense of peace, we are able to live fully, even while we are dying, because we realize the truth of the prayer of St. Francis of Assisi, "that it is in dying that we are born to eternal life."

### Involving the Family, the Mortuary, the Cemetery and the Parish Church

When the death of a loved one has occurred, the wishes of the deceased regarding the funeral plans should be reviewed, for example, using the forms found at the end of this booklet if they have been prepared in advance (pp. 47-56).

Then the parish, the mortuary and the cemetery should be contacted. Many cemeteries and mortuaries will contact the parish as plans are being made, but it is still advisable to contact the parish yourself. A date, time and place for both the funeral liturgy and the burial need to be established in collaboration with the parish, the cemetery and the mortuary.

Once the date for the funeral and final disposition of the body is set, this then gives the parties time to carry out their tasks. The parish can schedule the church for the funeral, arrange for musicians, prepare for a reception, etc. The mortuary will prepare the body for the funeral and for the final disposition. The cemetery can prepare the plot or mausoleum or the niche for the cremated remains. Meanwhile, the family is given time to notify their relatives and friends and make travel arrangements if necessary.

When making arrangements with the parish staff or planning team, there will be many decisions to make about the funeral liturgy. The parish is primarily responsible for scheduling and planning the liturgy, which includes such things as the selection of scripture readings and designation of readers, the selection of music and musicians, the eulogist and many other details about the ceremony. The parish, in turn, gives all that information to the mortuary after the planning session. The form in this booklet for the parish church (p. 55) will help to keep track of the many details that must be considered for celebrating the funeral liturgy.

When making arrangements with the cemetery, there will be important decisions about the final disposition of the body. Will the burial be in the ground in a plot and will there need to be a vault (a concrete form surrounding the casket), or will it be above ground in a mausoleum or crypt? If the body is to be cremated, will the cremated remains be buried in the ground or put in a special niche (a columbarium)? What will the burial marker or monument be?

When making arrangements with the mortuary, there will be decisions about the casket, obituary notices, prayer or memory cards, ushers, etc. The form in this booklet for the mortuary (p. 51) will be helpful for gathering most of the information that the mortuary will want to have.

After these initial planning sessions, the parish, the mortuary and the cemetery can begin their work. As the planning process unfolds, however, the family or persons responsible for planning the funeral should stay in contact with the parish, the mortuary and the cemetery to make sure that everything is proceeding smoothly and any problems that arise can be quickly resolved.

# Using Modern Technology and Social Media

*by Rev. Kenneth Koehler with Amy Sander Montanez and Dirk deVries*

Today's computer technology—coupled with social media like Facebook, Twitter and blogging—makes it easy and quick to communicate important information regarding any parish matter, including the death of a parishioner. How often haven't we heard: "I didn't know she passed away!" or "The funeral was *when?* Nobody told me!" The question is: How can we get the information to as many people as possible so that the right people know what they need to know, quickly and efficiently?

Social media and our connection to the world through our computers offer many useful ways to communicate such information. Most cell phones now have texting and email capabilities, so word can spread speedily and immediately. Most people have at least minimal Internet skills; many use Facebook and check it frequently. The notice about a death or a funeral can thus be shared very quickly.

Many churches themselves have the technology and staff to create and maintain their own Facebook pages, email lists and blogs; any and all of these can be effective ways to communicate the announcement of a death and the funeral arrangements to all members of the parish.

Ideally, your parish will already have established *clear policies* regarding the announcement of deaths and the details of funeral arrangements, *and* these policies will have been communicated so everyone in the parish knows what to expect, including how the announcement is made, what to communicate, when to say it, and to whom. If you're parish is large enough to have

a communications committee or department, they would be the natural ones to work out this policy and make sure all in the parish are aware of it. If you don't have one, now's the time to develop one!

In regard to funerals, the family of the deceased needs to have input about *what* is to be communicated, as well as *when, how* and *to whom*. Some families may be sensitive about some unusual circumstances that need to be considered before moving ahead. But again, what is your parish's established policy? In some parishes, it's assumed that families will be contacted first and allowed to decide what means of communicating will be used, while in other parishes, announcements move ahead without consulting the family. As a church, decide how to handle these situations before they arise.

In regard to specifics about the funeral, a family may not have the money to place a notice in the newspaper. They will, therefore, choose Internet options to communicate these details. Many mortuaries also provide their own Web page to communicate details of funerals and the contact information for families. That same Web page will often offer a place for people to leave their condolences and prayers for the family or to share meaningful memories or experiences they have had with the deceased.

In the hours following a death, most often the family will contact one of the priests or a parish minister. There is usually a phone number on the office's phone answering menu that will put the family in touch with the correct person. The parish staff will want to make a personal contact to arrange a one-on-one visit, not only to comfort, but also to begin the process of planning for the funeral.

Most importantly, the parish will want to hold as a priority face-to-face communication with the family of the deceased before any action is taken. Despite the ease and advantages of today's electronic and social media options, there is no substitute for hugs, shared tears and the offer of practical, hands-on help. Don't allow electronic options (which, lacking the tone of voice, the personal touch, the look on the face, etc. can be misunderstood or misinterpreted) to take the place of our customary ways of communicating and offering support.

If the parish does not have the technology, ask the family if a Facebook, email or blog address can be left with the parish receptionist to be given to those who wish to express their condolences electronically and where they can periodically check for additional details about the upcoming funeral or memorial service. When the family meets with the liturgical planner or priest, they can arrange what they would like to be put in place. The goal: to support both the parish and the family, and to more effectively mobilize the parish community in sharing the family's grief, offering their support and celebrating the life of a fellow parishioner.

An additional helpful online resource is CaringBridge, which you'll find at *www.caringbridge.org*. This Internet site provides a place for families to set up a free, personal page when a family member is seriously ill and the prognosis is poor. Once people know that a family has established a CaringBridge account, friends, family members and parishioners who visit and register at CaringBridge page will

be automatically notified when the family has posted anything new to the site, including changes in the patient's physical status, how treatment is proceeding and when (if) the death occurs. Those who respond can, in turn, leave their own messages for the patient and the family. CaringBridge also offers online suggestions for helping both family and friends through the process of death and dying. After the death, CaringBridge can continue to be a place for friends and parishioners to check in on the family to see how they're doing in the process of grieving and healing.

And finally, in today's online world, it's important, as we look ahead to our own potential illness and eventual passing, to include the necessary online information in the forms provided at the end of this book. This includes not only email addresses for online accounts (banks, investments firms, etc.), but also your login name and your password, so that your survivors will be able to communicate regarding your accounts. Since the first edition of *Preparing a Catholic Funeral*, this has been a major change to how most of us go about our day-to-day business.

To conclude: your parish has a great opportunity to make use of the Internet and social media to communicate and to comfort when it comes to serious illness and death in the parish. Never forget, however, that electronic communication can only supplement the personal, not replace it!

## Planning a Funeral

*by Rev. Kenneth Koehler*

While some view funerals as simply the end of a person's life, the Catholic Church celebrates funeral rites as the culmination of the deceased person's incorporation into the paschal mystery of Christ's life, death and resurrection. The funeral liturgy witnesses to the fundamental Christian conviction that death is only the end of our earthly life but not the end of our spiritual life in relationship to God.

Staking our lives on the hope of resurrection assured to us by Jesus, we believe that our death is the doorway to a new way of living with God. Baptism celebrates the beginning of our life in Christ and our commitment to God's ways throughout our lives. The funeral ritual celebrates one's earthly life in faithful relationship with God and looks toward the promise of existence with God forever. The funeral, then, is both an important celebration of the deceased believer's life and an expression and reaffirmation of the faith of the community.

At the funeral liturgy, we bring the body of our loved one back to the church one last time. Just as he or she was welcomed at the church door on the day of baptism, washed free of sin in the font and clothed in the white robe of redemption, so now we welcome the body back into the church one final time. We sprinkle the casket with holy water and clothe it in the white cloth (pall)—a reminder of the baptismal garment.

### The Funeral Is a Celebration of the Parish Community

A Christian funeral is celebrated in three stages: the vigil (commonly called the wake), the funeral liturgy (usually Mass, but not always), and the committal or final disposition of the body or cremated remains.

### 1. A Vigil Service Prepares for the Funeral

The preferred preparation for the funeral is a vigil or "wake" (so-called from the traditional practice of staying awake to watch over the body of a dead person) celebrated on the night before. The vigil or wake is the time when the life of the deceased as God's gift to us is remembered. It is an opportunity for family members and others from the community to share the meaning of the life of the deceased as the gift and blessing that he or she was to each of them. The vigil should be given as much attention as the funeral itself in order to prepare participants who come to the funeral the next day to celebrate the life of the deceased.

The revised *Order of Christian Funerals* has formulated a ritual to celebrate the vigil in a more prayerful way. It includes a time to gather, to pray, to read scripture, to tell stories and to support those who are grieving. This gives everyone attending the opportunity to remember the person's life and recall the joys and sorrows through which the meaning of a Christian life emerges.

Traditionally, it has been the custom in many places to pray only the Rosary at the vigil service. Although the Rosary is an appropriate and worthy prayer for those who are grieving, simply praying the Rosary at the vigil should not replace the Church's fuller ritual developed for celebrating the vigil service.

Occasionally, there is also the request by loved ones to have the Rosary recited in church prior to the funeral. But praying the Rosary immediately before the funeral Mass is not appropriate because the liturgical rituals of arriving at the Church to celebrate the funeral require a different attention to those gathering and to the beginning of the funeral. If the family wishes to say the Rosary, they can do so at home or at the mortuary prior to arriving at the church.

## 2. The Funeral Liturgy

The funeral Mass should ordinarily be held in the parish where the deceased was a member. For most believers, the parish community is the focus for much of their Christian life and the usual place where people celebrate and deepen their faith. Here they find the support and sharing for their growth in faith and in commitment to a Christian life. When determining the place of the funeral, these factors should always be considered.

Even when there are few family members or friends of the deceased, the funeral is an important part of parish life. Celebrating it together can enhance the faith of the parish community and remind them of the connection of death with the paschal mystery of Christ's death and resurrection. Thus it is preferable to have the funeral in the parish church rather than at the mortuary. However, special circumstances do sometimes warrant that a funeral take place in the mortuary chapel.

### The Funeral May Be Celebrated with or without Mass

It is usually preferable that Mass be celebrated with the funeral, but a funeral without Mass is also acceptable. The Church's directives in the *Order of Christian Funerals* do not require that Mass be celebrated with the funeral. Those responsible for planning the funeral should be aware of who is gathering and how best to carry out the wishes of the deceased.

If those who are to participate in the funeral have little experience of Catholic ritual and would be more comfortable not celebrating the Eucharist, the planners should consider a funeral without Mass. A funeral ritual without a Mass still celebrates the mystery of God in life and in death and commends the deceased to God's care.

### Cremation and the Funeral Service

Cremation has been an acceptable alternative to ground burial or entombment for Catholics since 1963. However, some advice concerning how to conduct a funeral with cremation is important because some additional requirements need to be discussed and arranged. If the body is to be cremated, this can happen either before or after the vigil and funeral service.

If cremation is to take place before the vigil, then it would be preferable that all the family of the deceased first spend time in the presence of the body, especially if they may not have been present at the time of death. This gathering helps with the grieving process and is an important way to commend the person to the care of the Lord. Then cremation can take place.

The *Order of Christian Funerals* instructs that the cremated remains be brought to the church for the funeral. It is suggested that a picture of the deceased be placed beside the cremated remains for the funeral celebration.

If cremation is to take place after the funeral, the mortuary can provide a temporary casket to have the body present during the vigil service and the funeral. Mortuaries often use a special rental casket for these ceremonies and then do the actual cremation with a simpler container. When the funeral is complete, then cremation can take place.

When there is cremation, sometimes persons want their remains scattered at a favorite place. The Catholic Church discourages this practice and instructs that the cremated remains are not to be scattered openly but should be put in a grave, tomb or burial place for cremated remains to which people may return for remembrance and prayer. This practice reflects the Christian belief that these remains are not just ashes but the remains of a person created in God's image who will return in fullness when Christ raises the dead to life. This also allows the family to establish a place to return to in order to continue their remembrance and honor of the deceased.

### 3. The Committal or Final Disposition of the Body

The concluding rite of the Christian funeral is the committal, in which the Christian community celebrates its final act of loving care for the body of the deceased person. At the graveside, tomb or crematorium, the community relinquishes its hold on the body and lovingly turns it over to the community of saints. In committing the body to its final resting place in the consecrated ground of the cemetery, the community expresses its hope that the remains of the deceased, together with those of the other faithful who also lie there, will await together their bodily resurrection with Christ.

# Guidelines for Giving a Eulogy at a Funeral Mass

*Rev. Kenneth Koehler*

Many times, we are unaware of how blessed we have been by the life of the person we are remembering. The person we are remembering is a person who grew from their mistakes and learned the meaning of God in their life. Their life touched those around them so deeply that it made them better people and came to know God even more profoundly.

The purpose for a eulogy at the funeral Mass is to present to those assembled the faith life of the person we are remembering. More than anything, it is about what this person contributed to the faith life of their children, friends and family and to the parish they belonged to.

Following are some guidelines to assist you in preparing a eulogy that is fitting and appropriate for the funeral celebration.

The family stories, remembrances, favorite sports, etc. can be more appropriately shared at the vigil in the presence of the deceased on the evening before the funeral. It is at this time people can appreciate and remember who this person has been for them. It is a time to laugh and a time to cry over the wonderful *and* difficult times of this person's life.

The Eulogy is never to be more than 10 minutes long and should be presented by only *one* speaker. If a member of the family would not be able to give the eulogy, then the family can gather and formulate the material for someone else to read for them. There may be a time to share special poems and verses that are meaningful, which could also be shared at the vigil.

The eulogy should not include anything about bad jokes or sports interests but about what this person has meant to their children, family and friends in terms of their faith life.

It is very appropriate to share how this person lived their faith at home, in the community, at work and at Church. This includes the values that were taught through their life and commitments, how they were a person of integrity. They were a gift to the parish by their life and their modeling of their faith.

It is helpful to share where the person grew up, something about their own family and the family they now have.

The important aspect of the eulogy is to bring to this community celebrating the deceased's life our reason to celebrate our thanks for the gift of their life in our midst.

# The Vigil Service: Sharing the Reality of Life and Death

*by Dianne L. Josephson, RN, MSN, author, educator, consultant and Director of the Healing After Loss Ministry at St. Pius X Parish, El Paso, TX*

The vigil service (wake) provides an opportunity for the community of faith to come together, usually the evening before the funeral, to share the realities of life and death. By participating in a sacred ritual, they bring to consciousness the Christian dimension of death. As an important component of the *Order of Christian Funerals*, the vigil service allows people to come face-to-face with the reality of the death. It is a time for experiencing the pain, contemplating the meaning and fragility of life and wondering how life will go on without the person who has died. It also allows the survivors time to be with the remains of the loved one before the final rite of committal.

The ritual should be somewhat informal and varied. It should be much more than just praying the rosary, as was often the focus in the past. The vigil is a time to gather together, read and reflect on scripture readings, pray, share condolences, remember and celebrate the life of the loved one or friend. The vigil service is the appropriate time for a eulogy or for testimonies from family members and friends, coworkers and others about the life of the deceased, using favorite stories, reminiscences and even humor. The homily, which takes place during the funeral Mass (if included prior to committal), is more formal and focuses on the relationship of this death to the resurrection of Jesus. For the deceased, suffering and death are over and the transition to eternal life is now complete.

When a death is sudden, there is often little time for the fact of the situation to set in before the funeral. The survivors can be in a state of shock and disbelief. In order to comprehend death's reality, it may be advisable to have an open coffin at the vigil. Sometimes when the casket is closed, disbelief in the actuality of the death, and even fantasies, can develop. It can be important for a person to view the body—even touch it—to allow the mind and the body to come to terms with the reality of the death. Fantasies regarding the fact of death sometime occur when the death is violent or disfiguring, as often happens in automobile accidents or fires. One mother, for example, whose son was killed in a motorcycle accident, was not allowed to see his badly disfigured body. She never quite accepted that it was her son who had been killed and for years believed her missing son would return to her.

In general, children should be included in all aspects of the vigil and funeral. During this time of sadness and grief, children need to feel secure in the presence of the family and be involved in the rituals of mourning. They must, however, be prepared for what they will encounter—events such as seeing and hearing a parent cry or witnessing someone faint. It is also important not to leave children alone. If a parent cannot be with them, then someone else whom they know and trust should serve as their companion. If children do not want to attend the vigil or funeral, then take time to answer their questions and address their concerns. Explain death realistically and honestly so they can proceed with their own grieving processes. Concentrate on what is important to them and do not give more information than necessary at the time. If they are still reluctant, do not pressure or force them to attend.

Through its participation in the ritual of the vigil service, the faith community is able to grow in its understanding of the realities of life and death in relation to the promise of Jesus' resurrection to new life. Most of all, when people gather at the vigil, they not only share the burden of grief but also realize the words of the prophet Isaiah, which also described the healing ministry of Jesus:

> *The Spirit of the Lord God is upon me,*
>   *because the LORD has anointed me;*
> *He has sent me to bring glad tidings to the*
>   *lowly,*
> *to heal the brokenhearted...*
> *to comfort all who mourn...*

# The Importance of the Vigil

*by Anthony Haas, Pastoral Associate and Director of Music and Liturgy,*
*Most Precious Blood Parish, Denver, CO*

The Order of Christian Funerals functions as a series of rituals that bridges the gap between our earthly life and the community of heaven. The celebration of the vigil marks the first time that family and friends gather publicly following a death. It is a grace-filled opportunity for the community to gather and share memories of the deceased and to find and give support and hope to one another in the face of death.

The vigil celebration is simple in format, but can be very profound in its experience. The vigil can take place at the home of the deceased, a funeral home, another suitable place or the church. It is most commonly celebrated as a service of the word, but for individuals and communities experienced in praying the Liturgy of the Hours, praying the Office of the Dead is another option. The service of the word follows the traditional format of an entrance song, first reading, responsorial psalm, gospel reading, homily and intercessions.

At the conclusion of the vigil an opportunity is provided for a family member or friend to speak in remembrance of the deceased. While the Order of Christian Funerals only mentions one person giving a remembrance, pastoral experience, and sometimes cultural customs, encourages more or all people to share stories and memories, if time allows.

Professional advice, as well as our own pastoral practice, teach us that the act of grieving is a process that frequently involves action. In earlier generations when someone died the body of the deceased would be laid out in the home, and the community would respond by visiting, bringing food and preparing the body and the grave. Storytelling about the life of the deceased naturally took place. It was a healthy, normal and holistic way of beginning the grief process in order to come to terms with death and suffering in life. To encourage healthy grieving the vigil service can facilitate what was a common practice.

Giving the community the opportunity to share, remember, laugh and cry through death can enrich the funeral experience. Jesus was a gifted storyteller who shared the life of God through colorful narratives. Our lives are the same; they are a collection of stories and experiences. One of the great joys for Christian communities is to see how each person is a unique gift of God, a unique story of God. Our own experience of God is broadened when we see how God is active and alive, not only in our own life, but in the lives of others. Sadly not all stories are widely known. A family I know discovered some unknown stories about their husband and father at the funeral vigil. He worked as an engineer and was very humble about his work and accomplishments. At the vigil some of his work colleagues were there and shared how the deceased had invented parts that were critical to projects that they worked on and how some of these inventions remain standards in the industry. This was news to the family and without the sharing of stories this side of their father would never have been known to them.

For families who have deceased family members who were veterans, knowing and sharing the stories of sacrifice, courage, honor and valor and how those experiences shaped the life of their loved ones are important to remember and share with future generations.

I have been to a countless number of funerals where the deceased had a prolonged illness like cancer and people shared stories of how, even in the midst of great suffering, they were inspired by the courage, the positive attitude and love shared by the deceased and how that had impacted their own lives.

Years ago, I visited with a priest who worked on a Native American reservation. Vigils for funerals lasted for three to five days, where the community gathered each evening for a service followed by a potluck and the sharing of stories. While many of the deaths on the reservation were tragic in nature, the community celebrated each death with reverence, beauty, care and respect.

No matter how stories are shared, sharing stories is vital for the vigil. If time allows for only a few to give a remembrance, a reception afterwards can naturally lead to the sharing of more memories. The celebration of the vigil flows to the celebration of the funeral itself. It is at that point that the story of the deceased is connected with the larger story of the Church woven together in a unified story of a life lived and a person's welcome into the community of heaven.

# Seven Tips about what to Say and Do to Comfort Others

*by Steven V. Malec, BBA, NCBF, national speaker and Director of Bereavement Ministry for the Catholic Cemeteries Association in the Diocese of Cleveland, OH*

When comforting those who mourn, do not allow your own sense of helplessness to restrain you from reaching out to the bereaved. Recognize the therapeutic value of your presence. The Order of Christian Funerals tells us that "members of the community should console the mourners with words of faith and support and with acts of kindness" (#10). You can help a grieving person by:

### 1. Giving them your listening presence.
Support is based more on effective listening than on any words you may say.

### 2. Giving them permission to grieve and express their feelings.
Allow them to talk. Don't be afraid of their tears.

### 3. Remembering with them.
Share stories, memories and photos. Use the deceased loved one's name.

### 4. Offering continued support.
Visit, email, text, telephone and write them, especially around difficult days: birthdays, anniversaries, holidays or other special occasions.

### 5. Avoiding use of clichés.
Speak from your heart.

### 6. Offering practical help.
Cook a meal, take them to the store, library, cemetery, etc.

### 7. Praying with them.
Offer to attend church with them. Give them a book of poems and prayers.

Many times, simple acts can facilitate much healing.

# *Scripture Reading for Funerals*

Although any favorite scripture passage may be chosen, the following suggestions are particularly appropriate for expressing the Christian meaning of death. Choose one reading from each of the three categories: the first reading from the Old Testament or certain New Testament readings during the Easter season, a second reading from the non-gospel books and letters of the New Testament, and a reading from the gospels. For the shorter form of a reading, omit the part in the brackets.

## *First Reading: Old Testament*

*(Choose one to be read by an assigned reader.)*

### *1. 2 Maccabees 12:43-46*

Judas, the ruler of Israel, took up a collection among all his soldiers, amounting to two thousand silver drachmas, which he sent to Jerusalem to provide for an expiatory sacrifice. In doing this he acted in a very excellent and noble way, inasmuch as he had the resurrection of the dead in view; for if he were not expecting the fallen to rise again, it would have been useless and foolish to pray for them in death. But if he did this with a view to the splendid reward that awaits those who had gone to rest in godliness, it was a holy and pious thought. Thus he made atonement for the dead that they might be freed from this sin.

### *2. Job 19:1, 23-27a*

Job answered Bildad the Shuhite and said:
Oh, would that my words were written down!
    Would that they were inscribed in a record:
That with an iron chisel and with lead,
    they were cut in the rock for ever!
But as for me, I know that my Vindicator lives,
    and that he will at last stand forth upon

the dust;
Whom I myself shall see:
    my own eyes, not another's, shall
        behold him.
And from my flesh I shall see God;
    my inmost being is consumed with longing.

### *3. Wisdom 3:1-9 or 3:1-6, 9*

The souls of the just are in the hand of God,
    and no torment shall touch them.
They seemed, in the view of the foolish, to
        be dead;
    and their passing away was thought an
        affliction
    and their going forth from us,
        utter destruction.
But they are in peace.
For if before men, indeed, they be punished,
    yet is their hope full of immortality.
Chastised a little, they shall be greatly blessed,
    because God tried them
    and found them worthy of himself.
As gold in the furnace, he proved them,
    and as sacrificial offerings he took them
        to himself.

[In the time of their visitation they shall shine,
    and shall dart about as sparks
        through stubble.
They shall judge nations and rule over peoples,
    and the LORD shall be their King forever.]
Those who trust in him shall understand truth,
    and the faithful shall abide with him in love:
Because grace and mercy are with his holy ones,
    and his care is with his elect.

### *4. Wisdom 4:7-15*

The just man, though he die early,
    shall be at rest.
For the age that is honorable comes not
    with the passing of time,

nor can it be measured in terms of years.
Rather, understanding is the hoary crown for
men,
and an unsullied life, the attainment of old
age.
He who pleased God was loved;
he who lived among sinners was
transported—
Snatched away, lest wickedness pervert his mind
or deceit beguile his soul;
For the witchery of paltry things obscures what
is right
and the whirl of desire transforms the
innocent mind.
Having become perfect in a short while,
he reached the fullness of a long career;
for his soul was pleasing to the LORD,
therefore he sped him out of the midst of
wickedness.
But the people saw and did not understand,
nor did they take this into account.

### 5. Isaiah 25:6a, 7-9

On this mountain the LORD of hosts
will provide for all peoples.
On this mountain he will destroy
the veil that veils all peoples,
The web that is woven over all nations;
he will destroy death forever.
The Lord GOD will wipe away
the tears from all faces;
The reproach of his people he will remove from
the whole earth; for the LORD has spoken.

On that day it will be said:
"Behold our God, to whom we looked to
save us!
This is the LORD for whom we looked;
let us rejoice and be glad that he has saved
us!"

### 6. Lamentations 3:17-26

My soul is deprived of peace,
I have forgotten what happiness is;
I tell myself my future is lost,
all that I hoped for from the LORD.
The thought of my homeless poverty
is wormwood and gall.
Remembering it over and over
leaves my soul downcast within me.
But I will call this to mind,
as my reason to have hope:

The favors of the LORD are not exhausted,
his mercies are not spent;
They are renewed each morning,
so great is his faithfulness.
My portion is the LORD, says my soul;
therefore will I hope in him.
Good is the LORD to one who waits for him, to
the soul that seeks him;
It is good to hope in silence
for the saving help of the LORD.

### 7. Daniel 12:1-3

In those days, I, Daniel, mourned
and heard this word of the Lord:
At that time there shall arise
Michael, the great prince,
guardian of your people;
It shall be a time unsurpassed in distress
since nations began until that time.
At that time your people shall escape,
everyone who is found written in the book.

Many of those who sleep
in the dust of the earth shall awake;
Some shall live forever,
others shall be an everlasting horror
and disgrace.
But the wise shall shine brightly

like the splendor of the firmament,
And those who lead the many to justice
    shall be like the stars forever.

# First Reading:
# New Testament During
# The Season Of Easter

### 1. Acts 10:34-43 or 10:34-36, 42-43

Peter proceeded to speak, saying: "In truth, I see that God shows no partiality. Rather, in every nation whoever fears him and acts uprightly is acceptable to him. You know the word that he sent to the Israelites as he proclaimed peace through Jesus Christ, who is Lord of all, [what has happened all over Judea, beginning in Galilee after the baptism that John preached, how God anointed Jesus of Nazareth with the Holy Spirit and power. He went about doing good and healing all those oppressed by the devil, for God was with him. We are witnesses of all that he did both in the country of the Jews and in Jerusalem. They put him to death by hanging him on a tree. This man God raised on the third day and granted that he be visible, not to all the people, but to us, the witnesses chosen by God in advance, who ate and drank with him after he rose from the dead]. He commissioned us to preach to the people and testify that he is the one appointed by God as judge of the living and the dead. To him all the prophets bear witness, that everyone who believes in him will receive forgiveness of sins through his name."

### 2. Revelation 14:13

I, John, heard a voice from heaven say, "Write this: Blessed are the dead who die in the Lord from now on." "Yes," said the Spirit, "let them find rest from their labors, for their works accompany them."

### 3. Revelation 20:11–21:1

I, John, saw a large white throne and the one who was sitting on it. The earth and the sky fled from his presence and there was no place for them. I saw the dead, the great and the lowly, standing before the throne, and scrolls were opened. Then another scroll was opened, the book of life. The dead were judged according to their deeds, by what was written in the scrolls. The sea gave up its dead; then Death and Hades gave up their dead. All the dead were judged according to their deeds. Then Death and Hades were thrown into the pool of fire. (This pool of fire is the second death.) Anyone whose name was not found written in the book of life was thrown into the pool of fire.

Then I saw a new heaven and a new earth. The former heaven and the former earth had passed away, and the sea was no more.

### 4. Revelation 21:1-5a, 6b-7

I, John, saw a new heaven and a new earth. The former heaven and the former earth had passed away, and the sea was no more. I also saw the holy city, a new Jerusalem, coming down out of heaven from God, prepared as a bride adorned for her husband. I heard a loud voice from the throne saying, "Behold, God's dwelling is with the human race. He will dwell with them and they will be his people and God himself will always be with them as their God. He will wipe every tear from their eyes, and there shall be no more death or mourning, wailing or pain, for the old order has passed away."

The One who sat on the throne said, "Behold, I make all things new. I am the Alpha and the Omega, the beginning and the end. To the thirsty I will give a gift from the spring of life-giving water. The victor will inherit these gifts, and I shall be his God, and he will be my son."

# Second Reading: New Testament

*(Choose one to be read by an assigned reader.)*

### 1. Romans 5:5-11

Brothers and sisters:

Hope does not disappoint, because the love of God has been poured out into our hearts through the Holy Spirit who has been given to us. For Christ, while we were still helpless, died at the appointed time for the ungodly. Indeed, only with difficulty does one die for a just person, though perhaps for a good person one might even find courage to die. But God proves his love for us in that while we were still sinners Christ died for us. How much more then, since we are now justified by his Blood, will we be saved through him from the wrath. Indeed, if, while we were enemies, we were reconciled to God through the death of his Son, how much more, once reconciled, will we be saved by his life. Not only that, but we also boast of God through our Lord Jesus Christ, through whom we have now received reconciliation.

### 2. Romans 5:17-21

Brothers and sisters:

If, by the transgression of one person, death came to reign through that one, how much more will those who receive the abundance of grace and of the gift of justification come to reign in life through the one Jesus Christ. In conclusion, just as through one transgression condemnation came upon all, so, through one righteous act, acquittal and life came to all. For just as through the disobedience of the one man the many were made sinners, so through the obedience of the one the many will be made righteous. The law entered in so that transgression might increase but, where sin increased, grace overflowed all the more, so that, as sin reigned in death, grace also might reign through justification for eternal life through Jesus Christ our Lord.

### 3. Romans 6:3-9 or 6:3-4, 8-9

Brothers and sisters:

Are you unaware that we who were baptized into Christ Jesus were baptized into his death? We were indeed buried with him through baptism into death, so that, just as Christ was raised from the dead by the glory of the Father, we too might live in newness of life.

[For if we have grown into union with him through a death like his, we shall also be united with him in the resurrection. We know that our old self was crucified with him, so that our sinful body might be done away with, that we might no longer be in slavery to sin. For a dead person has been absolved from sin.] If, then, we have died with Christ, we believe that we shall also live with him. We know that Christ, raised from the dead, dies no more; death no longer has power over him.

### 4. Romans 8:14-23

Brothers and sisters:

Those who are led by the Spirit of God are sons of God. For you did not receive a spirit of slavery to fall back into fear, but you received a spirit of adoption, through which we cry, "*Abba, Father!*" The Spirit itself bears witness with our spirit that we are children of God, and if children, then heirs, heirs of God and joint heirs with Christ, if only we suffer with him so that we may also be glorified with him.

I consider that the sufferings of this present time are as nothing compared with the glory to be revealed for us. For creation awaits with eager expectation the revelation of the children of God; for creation was made subject to futility, not of its own accord but because of the one who subjected it, in hope that creation itself would be set free from slavery to corruption and share in the glorious freedom of the children of God. We know that all creation is groaning in labor pains even until now; and not only that, but we ourselves, who have the firstfruits of the Spirit, we also groan within ourselves as we wait for adoption, the redemption of our bodies.

### 5. Romans 8:31b-35, 37-39

Brothers and sisters:
If God is for us, who can be against us? He who did not spare his own Son but handed him over for us all, how will he not also give us everything else along with him? Who will bring a charge against God's chosen ones? It is God who acquits us. Who will condemn? It is Christ Jesus who died, rather, was raised, who also is at the right hand of God, who indeed intercedes for us. What will separate us from the love of Christ? Will anguish, or distress, or persecution, or famine, or nakedness, or peril, or the sword?

No, in all these things we conquer overwhelmingly through him who loved us. For I am convinced that neither death, nor life, nor angels, nor principalities, nor present things, nor future things, nor powers, nor height, nor depth, nor any other creature will be able to separate us from the love of God in Christ Jesus our Lord.

### 6. Romans 14:7-9, 10c-12

Brothers and sisters:
No one of us lives for oneself, and no one dies for oneself. For if we live, we live for the Lord, and if we die, we die for the Lord; so then, whether we live or die, we are the Lord's. For this is why Christ died and came to life, that he might be Lord of both the dead and the living.

Why then do you judge your brother? Or you, why do you look down on your brother? For we shall all stand before the judgment seat of God; for it is written:

> As I live, says the Lord, every knee shall bend before me
> and every tongue shall give praise to God.

So then each of us shall give an account of himself to God.

### 7. I Corinthians 15:20-28 or 15:20-23

Brothers and sisters:
Christ has been raised from the dead, the firstfruits of those who have fallen asleep. For since death came through a man, the resurrection of the dead came also through a man. For just as in Adam all die, so too in Christ shall all be brought to life, but each one in proper order: Christ the firstfruits; then, at his coming, those who belong to Christ; [then comes the end, when he hands over the Kingdom to his God and Father. For he must reign until he has put all his enemies under his feet. The last enemy to be destroyed is death, *"for he subjected everything under his feet."* But when it says that everything has been subjected, it is clear that it excludes the one who subjected everything to him. When everything is subjected to him, then the Son himself will also be subjected to the one who subjected everything to him, so that God may be all in all].

### 8. I Corinthians 15:51-57

Brothers and sisters:
Behold, I tell you a mystery. We shall not all fall asleep, but we will all be changed, in an instant, in the blink of an eye, at the last trumpet. For the trumpet will sound, the dead will be raised incorruptible, and we shall be changed. For that which is corruptible must clothe itself with

incorruptibility, and that which is mortal must clothe itself with immortality. And when that which is corruptible clothes itself with incorruptibility and that which is mortal clothes itself with immortality, then the word that is written shall come about:

> Death is swallowed up in victory.
> Where, O death, is your victory?
> Where, O death, is your sting?

The sting of death is sin and the power of sin is the law. But thanks be to God who gives us the victory through our Lord Jesus Christ.

### 9. 2 Corinthians 4:14–5:1

Brothers and sisters:
Knowing that the One who raised the Lord Jesus will raise us also with Jesus and place us with you in his presence. Everything indeed is for you, so that the grace bestowed in abundance on more and more people may cause the thanksgiving to overflow for the glory of God. Therefore, we are not discouraged; rather, although our outer self is wasting away, our inner self is being renewed day by day. For this momentary light affliction is producing for us an eternal weight of glory beyond all comparison, as we look not to what is seen but to what is unseen; for what is seen is transitory, but what is unseen is eternal.

For we know that if our earthly dwelling, a tent, should be destroyed, we have a building from God, a dwelling not made with hands, eternal in heaven.

### 10. 2 Corinthians 5:1, 6-10

Brothers and sisters:
We know that if our earthly dwelling, a tent, should be destroyed, we have a building from God, a dwelling not made with hands, eternal in heaven.

We are always courageous, although we know that while we are at home in the body we are away from the Lord, for we walk by faith, not by sight. Yet we are courageous, and we would rather leave the body and go home to the Lord. Therefore, we aspire to please him, whether we are at home or away. For we must all appear before the judgment seat of Christ, so that each one may receive recompense according to what he did in the body, whether good or evil.

### 11. Philippians 3:20-21

Brothers and sisters:
Our citizenship is in heaven, and from it we also await a savior, the Lord Jesus Christ. He will change our lowly body to conform with his glorified Body by the power that enables him also to bring all things into subjection to himself.

### 12. 1 Thessalonians 4:13-18

We do not want you to be unaware, brothers and sisters, about those who have fallen asleep, so that you may not grieve like the rest who have no hope. For if we believe that Jesus died and rose, so too will God, through Jesus, bring with him those who have fallen asleep. Indeed, we tell you this on the word of the Lord, that we who are alive, who are left until the coming of the Lord, will surely not precede those who have fallen asleep. For the Lord himself, with a word of command, with the voice of an archangel and with the trumpet of God, will come down from heaven, and the dead in Christ will rise first. Then we who are alive, who are left, will be caught up together with them in the clouds to meet the Lord in the air. Thus we shall always be with the Lord. Therefore, console one another with these words.

### 13. 2 Timothy 2:8-13

Beloved:

Remember Jesus Christ, raised from the dead, a descendant of David: such is my Gospel, for which I am suffering, even to the point of chains, like a criminal. But the word of God is not chained. Therefore, I bear with everything for the sake of those who are chosen, so that they too may obtain the salvation that is in Christ Jesus, together with eternal glory. This saying is trustworthy:

> If we have died with him,
>   we shall also live with him;
> if we persevere,
>   we shall also reign with him.
> But if we deny him,
>   he will deny us.
> If we are unfaithful,
>   he remains faithful
>   for he cannot deny himself.

### 14. 1 John 3:1-2

Beloved:

See what love the Father has bestowed on us that we may be called the children of God. Yet so we are. The reason the world does not know us is that it did not know him. Beloved, we are God's children now; what we shall be has not yet been revealed. We do know that when it is revealed we shall be like him, for we shall see him as he is.

### 15. 1 John 3:14-16

Beloved:

We know that we have passed from death to life because we love our brothers. Whoever does not love remains in death. Everyone who hates his brother is a murderer, and you know that no murderer has eternal life remaining in him. The way we came to know love was that he laid down his life for us; so we ought to lay down our lives for our brothers.

# The Gospel

*(Choose one to be read by the priest.)*

### 1. Matthew 5:1-12a

When Jesus saw the crowds, he went up the mountain, and after he had sat down, his disciples came to him. He began to teach them, saying:

> "Blessed are the poor in spirit,
>   for theirs is the Kingdom of heaven.
> Blessed are they who mourn,
>   for they will be comforted.
> Blessed are the meek,
>   for they will inherit the land.
> Blessed are they who hunger and thirst for
>     righteousness,
>   for they will be satisfied.
> Blessed are the merciful,
>   for they will be shown mercy.
> Blessed are the clean of heart,
>   for they will see God.
> Blessed are the peacemakers,
>   for they will be called children of God.
> Blessed are they who are persecuted for the
>     sake of righteousness,
>   for theirs is the Kingdom of heaven.
> Blessed are you when they insult you and
>     persecute you
>   and utter every kind of evil against you
>     falsely because of me.
> Rejoice and be glad,
>   for your reward will be great in heaven."

### 2. Matthew 11:25-30

At that time Jesus answered: "I give praise to you, Father, Lord of heaven and earth, for although you have hidden these things from the wise and the learned you have revealed them to the childlike. Yes, Father, such has been your gracious will. All things have been handed over to me by my Father. No one knows the Son except the Father, and no one know the Father except the Son and anyone to whom the Son wishes to reveal him.

"Come to me, all you who labor and are burdened, and I will give you rest. Take my yoke upon you and learn from me, for I am meek and humble of heart; and you will find rest for yourselves. For my yoke is easy, and my burden light."

### 3. Matthew 25:1-13

Jesus told his disciples this parable:
"The Kingdom of heaven will be like ten virgins who took their lamps and went out to meet the bridegroom. Five of them were foolish and five were wise. The foolish ones, when taking their lamps, brought no oil with them, but the wise brought flasks of oil with their lamps. Since the bridegroom was long delayed, they all became drowsy and fell asleep. At midnight, there was a cry, 'Behold, the bridegroom! Come out to meet him!' Then all those virgins got up and trimmed their lamps. The foolish ones said to the wise, 'Give us some of your oil, for our lamps are going out.' But the wise ones replied, 'No, for there may not be enough for us and you. Go instead to the merchants and buy some for yourselves.' While they went off to buy it, the bridegroom came and those who were ready went into the wedding feast with him. Then the door was locked. Afterwards the other virgins came and said, 'Lord, Lord, open the door for us!' But he said in reply, 'Amen, I say to you, I do not know you.' Therefore, stay awake, for you know neither the day nor the hour."

### 4. Matthew 25:31-46

Jesus said to his disciples:
"When the Son of Man comes in his glory, and all the angels with him, he will sit upon his glorious throne and all the nations will be assembled before him. And he will separate them one from another, as a shepherd separates the sheep from the goats. He will place the sheep on his right and the goats on his left. Then the king will say to those on his right, 'Come, you who are blessed by my Father. Inherit the kingdom prepared for you from the foundation of the world. For I was hungry and you gave me food, I was thirsty and you gave me drink, a stranger and you welcomed me, naked and you clothed me, ill and you cared for me, in prison and you visited me.' Then the righteous will answer them and say, 'Lord, when did we see you hungry and feed you, or thirsty and give you drink? When did we see you a stranger and welcome you, or naked and clothe you? When did we see you ill or in prison, and visit you?' And the king will say to them in reply, 'Amen, I say to you, whatever you did for one of these least brothers of mine, you did for me.' Then he will say to those on his left, 'Depart from me, you accursed, into the eternal fire prepared for the Devil and his angels. For I was hungry and you gave me no food, I was thirsty and you gave me no drink, a stranger and you gave me no welcome, naked and you gave me no clothing, ill and in prison, and you did not care for me.' Then they will answer and say, 'Lord, when did we see you hungry or thirsty or a stranger or naked or ill or in prison, and not minister to your needs?' He will answer them, 'Amen, I say to you, what you did not do for one of these least ones, you did not do for me.' And these will go off to eternal punishment, but the righteous to eternal life."

### 5. Mark 15:33-39; 16:1-6 or 15:33-39

At noon darkness came over the whole land until three in the afternoon. And at three o'clock Jesus cried out in a loud voice, *"Eloi, Eloi, lema sabachthani?"* which is translated, "My God, my God, why have you forsaken me?" Some of the bystanders who heard it said, "Look, he is calling Elijah." One of them ran, soaked a sponge with wine, put it on a reed, and gave it to him to drink, saying, "Wait, let us see if Elijah comes to take him down." Jesus gave a loud cry and breathed his last. The veil of the sanctuary was torn in two from top to bottom. When the centurion who stood facing him saw how he breathed his last he said, "Truly this man was the Son of God!"

[When the sabbath was over, Mary Magdalene, Mary, the mother of James, and Salome bought spices so that they might go and anoint him. Very early when the sun had risen, on the first day of the week, they came to the tomb. They were saying to one another, "Who will roll back the stone for us from the entrance to the tomb?" When they looked up, they saw that the stone had been rolled back; it was very large. On entering the tomb they saw a young man sitting on the right side, clothed in a white robe, and they were utterly amazed. He said to them, "Do not be amazed! You seek Jesus of Nazareth, the crucified. He has been raised; he is not here. Behold the place where they laid him."]

### 6. Luke 7:11-17

Jesus journeyed to a city called Nain, and his disciples and a large crowd accompanied him. As he drew near to the gate of the city, a man who had died was being carried out, the only son of his mother, and she was a widow. A large crowd from the city was with her. When the Lord saw her, he was moved with pity for her and said to her, "Do not weep." He stepped forward and touched the coffin; at this the bearers halted, and he said, "Young man, I tell you, arise!" The dead man sat up and began to speak, and Jesus gave him to his mother. Fear seized them all, and they glorified God, exclaiming, "A great prophet has arisen in our midst," and "God has visited his people." This report about him spread through the whole of Judea and in all the surrounding region.

### 7. Luke 12:35-40

Jesus said to his disciples:
"Gird your loins and light your lamps and be like servants who await their master's return from a wedding, ready to open immediately when he comes and knocks. Blessed are those servants whom the master finds vigilant on his arrival. Amen, I say to you, he will gird himself, have them recline at table, and proceed to wait on them. And should he come in the second or third watch and find them prepared in this way, blessed are those servants. Be sure of this: if the master of the house had known the hour when the thief was coming, he would not have let his house be broken into. You also must be prepared, for at an hour you do not expect, the Son of Man will come."

### 8. Luke 23:33, 39-43

When they came to the place called the Skull, they crucified Jesus and the criminals there, one on his right, the other on his left.

Now one of the criminals hanging there reviled Jesus, saying, "Are you not the Christ? Save yourself and us." The other, however, rebuking him, said in reply, "Have you no fear of God, for you are subject to the same condemnation? And indeed, we have been condemned justly, for the sentence we received corresponds to our crimes, but this man has done nothing criminal." Then he said, "Jesus, remember me when you come into your Kingdom." He replied to him, "Amen, I say to you, today you will be with me in Paradise."

### 9. Luke 23:44-46, 50, 52-53; 24:1-6a or 44-46, 50, 52-53

It was now about noon and darkness came over the whole land until three in the afternoon because of an eclipse of the sun. Then the veil of the temple was torn down the middle. Jesus cried out in a loud voice, "Father, into your hands I commend my spirit"; and when he had said this, he breathed his last.

Now there was a virtuous and righteous man named Joseph who, though he was a member of the council, he went to Pilate and asked for the Body of Jesus. After he had taken the Body down, he wrapped it in a linen cloth and laid him in a rock-hewn tomb in which no one had yet been buried.

[But at daybreak on the first day of the week, the women took the spices they had prepared and went to the tomb. They found the stone rolled away from the tomb; but when they entered, they did not find the Body of the Lord Jesus. While they were puzzling over this, behold, two men in dazzling garments appeared to them. They were terrified and bowed their faces to the ground. They said to them, "Why do you seek the living one among the dead? He is not here, but he has been raised."]

### 10. Luke 24:13-35 or 24:13-16, 28-35

That very day, the first day of the week, two of the disciples were going to a village called Emmaus seven miles from Jerusalem, and they were conversing about all the things that had occurred. And it happened that while they were conversing and debating, Jesus himself drew near and walked with them, but their eyes were prevented from recognizing him. [He asked them, "What are you discussing as you walk along?" They stopped, looking downcast. One of them, named Cleopas, said to him in reply, "Are you the only visitor to Jerusalem who does not know of the things that have taken place there in these days?" And he replied to them, "What sort of things?" They said to him, "The things that happened to Jesus the Nazarene, who was a prophet mighty in deed and word before God and all the people, how our chief priests and rulers both handed him over to a sentence of death and crucified him. But we were hoping that he would be the one to redeem Israel; and besides all this, it is now the third day since this took place. Some women from our group, however, have astounded us: they were at the tomb early in the morning and did not find his Body; they came back and reported that they had indeed seen a vision of angels who announced that he was alive. Then some of those with us went to the tomb and found things just as the women had described, but him they did not see." And he said to them, "Oh, how foolish you are! How slow of heart to believe all that the prophets spoke! Was it not necessary that the Christ should suffer these things and enter into his glory?" Then beginning with Moses and all the prophets, he interpreted to them what referred to him in all the Scriptures.] As they approached the village to which they were going, he gave the impression that he was going farther. But they urged him, "Stay with us, for it is nearly evening and the day is almost over." So he went in to stay with them. And it happened that, while he was with them at table, he took bread, said the blessing, broke it, and gave it to them. With that their eyes were opened and they recognized him, but he vanished from their sight. Then they said to each other, "Were not our hearts burning within us while he spoke to us on the way and opened the Scriptures to us?" So they set out at once and returned to Jerusalem where they found gathered together the Eleven and those with them who were saying, "The Lord has truly been raised and has appeared to Simon!" Then the two recounted what had taken place on the way and how he was made known to them in the breaking of the bread.

### 11. John 5:24-29

Jesus answered the Jews and said to them: "Amen, amen, I say to you, whoever hears my word and believes in the one who sent me has eternal life and will not come to condemnation, but has passed from death to life. Amen, amen, I say to you, the hour is coming and is now here when the dead will hear the voice of the Son of God, and those who hear will live. For just as the Father has life in himself, so also he gave to his Son the possession of life in himself. And he gave him power to exercise judgment, because he is the Son of Man. Do not be amazed at this, because the hour is coming in which all who are in the tombs will hear his voice and will come out, those who have done good deeds to the resurrection of life, but those who have done wicked deeds to the resurrection of condemnation."

### 12. John 6:37-40

Jesus said to the crowds: "Everything that the Father gives me will come to me, and I will not reject anyone who comes to me, because I came down from heaven not to do my own will but the will of the one who sent me. And this is the will of the one who sent me,

that I should not lose anything of what he gave me, but that I should raise it on the last day. For this is the will of my Father, that everyone who sees the Son and believes in him may have eternal life, and I shall raise him on the last day."

### 13. John 6:51-58

Jesus said to the crowds: "I am the living bread that came down from heaven; whoever eats this bread will live forever; and the bread that I will give is my Flesh for the life of the world."

The Jews quarreled among themselves, saying, "How can this man give us his Flesh to eat?" Jesus said to them, "Amen, amen, I say to you, unless you eat the Flesh of the Son of Man and drink his Blood, you do not have life within you. Whoever eats my Flesh and drinks my Blood has eternal life, and I will raise him on the last day. For my Flesh is true food, and my Blood is true drink. Whoever eats my Flesh and drinks my Blood remains in me and I in him. Just as the living Father sent me and I have life because of the Father, so also the one who feeds on me will have life because of me. This is the bread that came down from heaven. Unlike your ancestors who ate and still died, whoever eats this bread will live forever."

### 14. John 11:17-27 or 11:21-27

[When Jesus arrived in Bethany he found that Lazarus had already been in the tomb for four days. Now Bethany was near Jerusalem, only about two miles away. And many of the Jews had come to Martha and Mary to comfort them about their brother. When Martha heard that Jesus was coming, she went to meet him; but Mary sat at home.] Martha said to Jesus, "Lord, if you had been here, my brother would not have died. But even now I know that whatever you ask of God, God will give you." Jesus said to her, "Your brother will rise." Martha said to him, "I know he will rise, in the resurrection on the last day." Jesus told her, "I am the resurrection and the life; whoever believes in me, even if he dies, will live, and everyone who lives and believes in me will never die. Do you believe this?" She said to him, "Yes, Lord. I have come to believe that you are the Christ, the Son of God, the one who is coming into the world."

### 15. *John 11:32-45*

When Mary came to where Jesus was and saw him, she fell at his feet and said to him, "Lord, if you had been here, my brother would not have died." When Jesus saw her weeping and the Jews who had come with her weeping, he became perturbed and deeply troubled, and said, "Where have you laid him?" They said to him, "Sir, come and see." And Jesus wept. So the Jews said, "See how he loved him." But some of them said, "Could not the one who opened the eyes of the blind man have done something so that this man would not have died?"

So Jesus, perturbed again, came to the tomb. It was a cave, and a stone lay across it. Jesus said, "Take away the stone." Martha, the dead man's sister, said to him, "Lord, by now there will be a stench; he has been dead for four days." Jesus said to her, "Did I not tell you that if you believe you will see the glory of God?" So they took away the stone. And Jesus raised his eyes and said, "Father, I thank you for hearing me. I know that you always hear me; but because of the crowd here I have said this, that they may believe that you sent me." And when he had said this, he cried out in a loud voice, "Lazarus, come out!" The dead man came out, tied hand and foot with burial bands, and his face was wrapped in a cloth. So Jesus said to them, "Untie him and let him go."

Now many of the Jews who had come to Mary and seen what he had done began to believe in him.

### 16. *John 12:23-28 or 12:23-26*

Jesus said to his disciples:
"The hour has come for the Son of Man to be glorified. Amen, amen, I say to you, unless a grain of wheat falls to the ground and dies, it remains just a grain of wheat; but if it dies, it produces much fruit. Whoever loves his life loses it, and whoever hates his life in this world will preserve it for eternal life. Whoever serves me must follow me, and where I am, there also will my servant be. The Father will honor whoever serves me.

["I am troubled now. Yet what should I say? 'Father, save me from this hour'? But it was for this purpose that I came to this hour. Father, glorify your name.'"Then a voice came from heaven, "I have glorified it and will glorify it again."]

### 17. *John 14:1-6*

Jesus said to his disciples:
"Do not let your hearts be troubled. You have faith in God; have faith also in me. In my Father's house there are many dwelling places. If there were not, would I have told you that I am going to prepare a place for you? And if I go and prepare a place for you, I will come back again and take you to myself, so that where I am you also may be. Where I am going you know the way." Thomas said to him, "Master, we do not know where you are going; how can we know the way?"Jesus said to him, "I am the way and the truth and the life. No one comes to the Father except through me."

### 18. John: 17:24-26

Jesus raised his eyes to heaven and said: "Father, those whom you gave me are your gift to me. I wish that where I am they also may be with me, that they may see my glory that you gave me, because you loved me before the foundation of the world. Righteous Father, the world also does not know you, but I know you, and they know that you sent me. I made known to them your name and I will make it known, that the love with which you loved me may be in them and I in them."

### 19. John: 19:17-18, 25-39

So they took Jesus, and, carrying the cross himself, he went out to what is called the Place of the Skull, in Hebrew, Golgotha. There they crucified him, and with him two others, one on either side, with Jesus in the middle.

Standing by the cross of Jesus were his mother and his mother's sister, Mary the wife of Clopas, and Mary Magdalene. When Jesus saw his mother and the disciple there whom he loved, he said to his mother, "Woman, behold, your son." Then he said to the disciple, "Behold, your mother." And from that hour the disciple took her into his home.

After this, aware that everything was now finished, in order that the Scripture might be fulfilled, Jesus said, "I thirst." There was a vessel filled with common wine. So they put a sponge soaked in wine on a sprig of hyssop and put it up to his mouth. When Jesus had taken the wine, he said, "It is finished." And bowing his head, he handed over the Spirit.

Now since it was preparation day, in order that the bodies might not remain on the cross on the sabbath, for the sabbath day of that week was a solemn one, the Jews asked Pilate that their legs be broken and that they be taken down. So the soldiers came and broke the legs of the first and then of the other one who was crucified with Jesus. But when they came to Jesus and saw that he was already dead, they did not break his legs, but one soldier thrust his lance into his side, and immediately blood and water flowed out. An eyewitness has testified, and his testimony is true; he knows that he is speaking the truth, so that you also may come to believe. For this happened so that the Scripture passage might be fulfilled:

*Not a bone of it will be broken.*

And again another passage says:

*They will look upon him whom they have pierced.*

After this, Joseph of Arimathea, secretly a disciple of Jesus for fear of the Jews, asked Pilate if he could remove the body of Jesus. And Pilate permitted it. So he came and took his body. Nicodemus, the one who had first come to him at night, also came bringing a mixture of myrrh and aloes weighing about one hundred pounds.

# *Music Suggestions for Funerals*

Below are listed the titles for some of the many songs that are appropriate for funeral liturgies. Music that is not appropriate for a worship service may be selected for the vigil or wake of the deceased. There may be justifiable reasons to select nonworship music for the funeral service but this must be arranged with the parish planning team or priest presiding at the funeral. Your parish liturgist or music minister will be able to help you find music for your selections.

### *Gathering Songs*

Be Not Afraid (Dufford) OCP & GIA

Christ the Lord Is Risen Today (Wesley/ Williams) OCP & GIA

Covenant Hymn (Daigle/Cooney) GIA

Crown Him with Many Crowns (Elvey/Bridges) OCP & GIA

Hosea (Norbert) OCP & GIA

I Know that My Redeemer Lives (Hatton/ Medley) GIA

I Know that My Redeemer Lives (Soper) OCP

I Know that My Redeemer Lives (Haas) GIA

Jesus Christ Is Risen Today (traditional) OCP & GIA

On Eagle's Wings (Joncas) OCP & GIA

Remember Your Love (Ducote/Daigle) Damean Music distributed by OCP & GIA

You Are Mine (Haas) OCP & GIA

### *Responsorial Psalms*

Ps. 23: Shepherd Me O God (Haugen) OCP & GIA

Ps. 23: The Lord Is My Shepherd (Alstott) OCP

Ps. 25: To You, O Lord (Haugen) GIA

Ps. 25: To You, O Lord (Soper) OCP

Ps. 27: The Goodness of the Lord (Soper) OCP

Ps. 27: The Lord Is My Light (Haas) GIA

Ps. 34: The Cry of the Poor (Foley) OCP & GIA

Ps. 34: I Will Bless the Lord (Gouin) GIA

Ps. 34: Taste and See (Haugen) GIA

Ps. 34: Taste and See (Talbot) OCP

Ps. 34: Taste and See (Hurd) OCP

Ps. 63: My Soul Is Thirsting (Feiten) EKKLESIA Music, Inc.

Ps. 84: Happy Are They (Porter) GIA

Ps. 91: Be with Me, Lord (Joncas) OCP

Ps. 91: Be with Me, Lord (Haugen) GIA

Ps. 103: Forget Not What God Has Done (Haugen) GIA

Ps. 103: The Lord Is Kind and Merciful (Haugen) GIA

Ps 122: Let Us Go Rejoicing (Haugen) GIA

Ps. 122: Let Us Go Rejoicing (Joncas) GIA

Ps 145: 1 Will Praise Your Name (Haas) GIA

### *Preparation of the Gifts*

Holy Darkness (Schutte) OCP

In the Shadow of Your Wings (O'Connor) New Dawn Music

Only This I Want (Schutte) OCP, GIA & New Dawn Music

Out of the Depths (Raffa) EKKLESIA Music, Inc.

Precious in Your Sight (Raffa) EKKLESIA Music, Inc.

Precious Lord, Take My Hand (Allen/Dorsey) OCP

Restless Is the Heart (Farrell) OCP

Shepherd of My Heart (O'Brien) GIA

Shelter Me, O God (Hurd) OCP & GIA

The King of Love My Shepherd Is (traditional Irish melody) OCP & GIA

We Have Been Told (Haas) OCP & GIA

What Wondrous Love Is This (traditional) OCP & GIA

## Communion Songs

Behold the Lamb (Willett) OCP & GIA

Blest Are They (Haas) OCP & GIA

Bread of Life (Cooney) OCP

Eye Has Not Seen (Haugen) OCP & GIA

I Am the Bread of Life (Toolan) OCP & GIA

Give Me Jesus (spiritual/Hansen) OCP

Keep in Mind (Deiss) World Library Publications, Inc.

Now We Remain (Haas) OCP & GIA

Seed, Scattered and Sown (Feiten) OCP & GIA

Song of the Body of Christ (Haas) OCP & GIA

Take and Eat (Joncas/Quinn) GIA

Taste and See (Moore) OCP & GIA

Unless a Grain of Wheat (Farrell) OCP & GIA

We Walk by Faith (Shanti/Haugen/Alford) OCP & GIA

Without Seeing You (Haas) GIA

You Are Near (Schutte) OCP & GIA

## Songs of Farewell

*In Paradisum*/May Angels Guide You (chant/Alstott) OCP & GIA

May the Angels Lead You into Paradise (Hughes) GIA

Song of Farewell (Old One Hundredth/ Smolarski) OCP

Song of Farewell (Sands) OCP

## Closing Songs

Amazing Grace (traditional/Newton)

How Great Thou Art (traditional/Hine) OCP & GIA

Jerusalem, My Happy Home (traditional) OCP & GIA

Prayer of St. Francis (Temple) OCP & GIA

Sing a New Song (Schutte) GIA

We Will Rise Again ( Haas) OCP & GIA

Ye Watchers and Ye Holy Ones (traditional/ Riley) GIA

Yes, I Shall Arise (Alstott) OCP

## Music Publishers

EKKLESIA MUSIC, Inc.
(303) 757-4853
www.ekklesiamusic.com

GIA Publications, Inc.
7404 So. Mason Ave.
Chicago, IL 60638
(800) GIA-1358 (442-1358)
www.giamusic.com/

Oregon Catholic Press (OCP)
5536 NE Hassalo
Portland, OR 97213-3638
1-(800) LITURGY (548-8749)
liturgy@ocp.org
www.ocp.org

World Library Publications
3708 River Road, Suite 400
Franklin Park, IL, 60131-2158
(800) 566-6150
www.wlpmusic.com
wlps@jspawch.com

# Vital Information for Survivors or Personal Representative

Name _____
       Last              First               Middle (or Initial)

Address _____
       Street                      City           State     Zip

Telephone _____ Email _____ Social Security # _____ _____ _____

Date of Birth _____ Place of Birth _____
                                                      City

Citizen of _____
                    Country

Resided in County for (how long) _____ in State (how long) _____

Single___ Married___ Widowed___ Divorced___ Separated___

Name of Spouse _____ Alive _____ Deceased _____

Wedding Date/Anniversary _____ Occupation and Title (or retired from) _____

Type of Business/Employer _____ How Long_____

Father _____ _____ _____
       Name                             Date of Birth       Birthplace

Mother _____ _____ _____
      Maiden Name                      Date of Birth       Birthplace

Persons to Notify: Next of Kin Other than Spouse

| Name | Address | Phone | Relationship |
|---|---|---|---|
| Email | Facebook | LinkedIn | Other |
| Name | Address | Phone | Relationship |
| Email | Facebook | LinkedIn | Other |
| Name | Address | Phone | Relationship |
| Email | Facebook | LinkedIn | Other |
| Name | Address | Phone | Relationship |
| Email | Facebook | LinkedIn | Other |

| Name | Address | Phone | Relationship |
|------|---------|-------|--------------|

| Email | Facebook | LinkedIn | Other |
|-------|----------|----------|-------|

| Name | Address | Phone | Relationship |
|------|---------|-------|--------------|

| Email | Facebook | LinkedIn | Other |
|-------|----------|----------|-------|

Other Persons/Organizations

Church _____ Phone _____

    Email _____ Website _____

Doctor _____ Phone _____

    Email _____ Website _____

Mortuary _____ Phone _____

    Email _____ Website _____

Personal Representative/Attorney _____ Phone _____

    Email _____ Website _____

Organizations

| Name | Address | Phone | Relationship |
|------|---------|-------|--------------|

| Email | Facebook | LinkedIn | Other |
|-------|----------|----------|-------|

| Name | Address | Phone | Relationship |
|------|---------|-------|--------------|

| Email | Facebook | LinkedIn | Other |
|-------|----------|----------|-------|

| Name | Address | Phone | Relationship |
|------|---------|-------|--------------|

| Email | Facebook | LinkedIn | Other |
|-------|----------|----------|-------|

| Name | Address | Phone | Relationship |
|------|---------|-------|--------------|

| Email | Facebook | LinkedIn | Other |
|-------|----------|----------|-------|

# Financial Papers & Records

Where Records Located _____ Social Security Number _____

## Will

I have a will. Yes _____ No _____ Will Dated _____ Where Located _____

Executor _____ Phone _____

     Email _____ Other _____

Attorney _____ Phone _____

     Email _____ Other _____

Additional Information _____

## Banking

     Bank _____ Phone _____

     Address _____

     Website _____ Login/User Name _____ Password _____

     Type of Account(s)  Checking # _____ Savings # _____ Other _____

     Bank _____ Phone _____

     Address _____

     Website _____ Login/User Name _____ Password _____

     Type of Account(s)  Checking # _____ Savings # _____ Other _____

## Safety Deposit Box _____

| Number | Key Location | Bank |
|---|---|---|
| Address | | Phone |

## Insurance Policies _____

| Name | Policy Number | Company/Union/Organization/Agent | |
|---|---|---|---|
| Phone | Website | User Name | Password |
| Email | | | |
| Name | Policy Number | Company/Union/Organization/Agent | |
| Phone | Website | User Name | Password |
| Email | | | |

# Financial Papers & Records (cont.)

**Pension/Investments**

Pension _____

           Name/Number       Administrator          Address

_____

           Website              User Name          Password

401/K Plan _____

           Name/Number       Administrator          Address

_____

           Website              User Name          Password

Investments _____

           Name/Number       Administrator          Address

_____

           Website              User Name          Password

_____

           Name/Number       Administrator          Address

_____

           Website              User Name          Password

Other Benefits

_____

           Name/Number       Administrator          Address

_____

           Website              User Name          Password

_____

           Name/Number       Administrator          Address

_____

           Website              User Name          Password

**Veteran Information**

Service Identification/Serial Number _____ Rank & Branch of Service_____

Location of Veteran's Office to Notify _____

                              Address                        Phone

Entered Service _____ Separated from Service _____

               Date/Place                                Date/Place

Wars Fought _____ Medals or Honors _____

I would want American flag for my family _____ and military honors (if available) _____

Any other instructions or information (especially any things you don't want to take place).

_____

_____

# *Vital Information for the Mortuary*

Name _____
    Last            First            Middle (or Initial)

Address _____
    Street                City            State        Zip

Telephone _____ Email _____ Social Security # _____ _____ _____

Date of Birth _____ Place of Birth _____
                                        City

Citizen of _____
                Country

Resided in County for (how long) _____ in State (how long) _____

Single____ Married____ Widowed____ Divorced____ Separated____

Name of Spouse _____ Alive _____ Deceased _____

Wedding Date/Anniversary _____ Occupation and Title (or retired from)

Type of Business/Employer _____ How Long_____

Father _____ _____ _____
        Name                        Date of Birth        Birthplace

Mother _____ _____ _____
        Maiden Name                    Date of Birth        Birthplace

## Veteran Information

Service Identification/Serial Number _____ Rank & Branch of Service _____

Location of Veteran's Office to Notify _____
                    Address                    Phone
Website _____ User Name _____ Password _____

Entered Service _____ Separated from Service _____
            Date/Place                        Date/Place

Wars Fought _____ Medals or Honors _____

I would want American flag for my family _____ and military honors (if available) _____

Floral Request _____ _____

Gifts   Instead of flowers, I would prefer that my friends make memorial gifts to

| Name | Address | Website |
|------|---------|---------|
| Name | Address | Website |
| Name | Address | Website |

Final Disposition of My Body  ( ) Burial   ( ) Cremation  ( ) Donation for Research

at: _____cemetery

I have ( ) or have not ( ) consulted with the above named cemetery regarding:  a cemetery plot ( )

a vault ( )   crypt ( )   niche for created remains ( )   memorial marker ( ) services and a casket ( )

The location or number of my burial plot (cemetery, mausoleum, columbarium niche) or other instructions is

_____I

I do wish ( )   I do not wish ( )   or ( ) let my family decide to have an open casket.

If open: Clothing _____ Jewelry _____ Glasses on ( ) off ( )

# *Funeral Services*

Type of Services

___ Evening Vigil Service with Morning Mass and Burial    ___ Morning Mass and Burial

___ Cremation, Memorial Mass Followed by Burial    ___ Evening Mass and Morning Burial

___ Funeral Mass Followed by Cremation and Burial of Ashes Later

___ Memorial Service Only without Mass    ___ Graveside Service Only

I want to have these services conducted at (  ) Church _____

(  ) Funeral Home _____ (  ) Other _____
                Date and time                                   Date and time

Clergy/Presider  1st Choice _____ 2nd Choice _____

Eulogist        1st Choice _____ 2nd Choice _____

Pallbearers     Name _____ Phone _____ Email _____

             Name _____ Phone _____ Email _____

             Name _____ Phone _____ Email _____

             Name _____ Phone _____ Email _____

Other specific instructions not covered above _____

## Vigil Service

Scripture Readings  1st Reading _____ Reader _____

                  2st Reading _____ Reader _____

                  3rd Reading _____ Reader _____

Other Favorite Prayer, Poem, Quote or Article (include a copy)

                    _____ Reader _____

                    _____ Reader _____

Music at Vigil Service _____ _____

                         _____ _____

## Funeral Mass

Scripture Readings  1st Reading _____ Reader _____

                  2nd Reading _____ Reader _____

                  The Gospel _____ Priest _____

Music    _____ _____

        _____ _____

Other specific directions not covered above: _____

_____

Signature _____ _____
               Signature               Date

Witnesses _____ _____ _____ _____
           Signature      Date         Signature      Date

*This page may be torn out, copied and put in with your will and important papers or given to your church or personal representative.*

# *Vital Information for the Parish Church*

Name _____
        Last                First              Middle (or Initial)

Address _____
        Street                  City          State     Zip

Telephone _____ Email _____ Social Security # _____ _____ _____

Date of Birth _____ Place of Birth _____
                                                      City

Citizen of _____
                   Country

Resided in County for (how long) _____ in State (how long) _____

Single____ Married____ Widowed____ Divorced____ Separated____

Name of Spouse _____ Alive _____ Deceased _____

Wedding Date/Anniversary _____ Occupation and Title (or retired from)

Type of Business/Employer _____ How Long_____

Father _____ _____ _____
        Name                          Date of Birth      Birthplace

Mother _____ _____ _____
        Maiden Name                   Date of Birth      Birthplace

## Veteran Information

Service Identification/Serial Number _____ Rank & Branch of Service _____

Location of Veteran's Office to Notify _____
                                  Address                     Phone
Website _____

Entered Service _____ Separated from Service _____
             Date/Place                                Date/Place

Wars Fought _____ Medals or Honors _____

Floral Request _____ _____

Gifts  Instead of flowers, I would prefer that my friends make memorial gifts to

| Name | Address | Website |
|------|---------|---------|
| Name | Address | Website |
| Name | Address | Website |

# Vital Information for the Parish Church (cont.)

Final Disposition of My Body   (  ) Burial   (  ) Cremation   (  ) Donation for Research

at: _____cemetery

I have (  ) or have not (  ) consulted with the above named cemetery regarding:  a cemetery plot (  )

a vault (  )    crypt (  )    niche for created remains (  )    memorial marker (  ) services and a casket (  )

The location or number of my burial plot (cemetery, mausoleum, columbarium niche) or other instructions is

_____I

I do wish (  )   I do not wish (  )   or (  ) let my family decide to have an open casket.

If open: Clothing _____ Jewelry _____ Glasses on (  ) off (  )